Hal Leonard Student Piano Library

Hanon for the Developing Pianist

Selections from *The Virtuoso Pianist*

Exercises based upon Charles-Louis Hanon's *The Virtuoso Pianist in 60 Exercises*, arranged and simplified for the developing pianist.

Margaret Otwell, Editor

Carol Klose and Jennifer Linn, Assistant Editors

About This Edition

In this new edition of Hanon's classic exercises for piano, some changes have been made to the original score to make the exercises more accessible for all students:

- Eighth notes are used in place of the original sixteenth notes.
- Each exercise has been shortened by half the original length.
- The R.H. and L.H. parts have been placed two octaves apart, so that students can maintain a more comfortable hand and arm position as they play.
- An *optional* break between the ascending and descending parts of each exercise has been added, so that students may learn the ascending part of an exercise thoroughly before going on to learn the descending part.

We have also added these original features:

- Preceding each exercise is a worksheet divided into three sections: **Practice Tips**, **Quick Quiz**, and **Virtuoso Variations**. These worksheets will help students focus on the important technical features in each exercise, apply practical music theory to their study of the music, and vary the exercises in creative ways.
- Following the first twenty exercises are eight chromatic-scale exercises based on those found in the original Schirmer edition of *The Virtuoso Pianist Book II.* These have been simplified in the same way as the preceding exercises.

Book: ISBN 978-0-634-03159-5

Book/Audio: ISBN 978-0-634-02992-9

T0048536

G. SCHIRMER, Inc.

DISTRIBUTED BY

HAL•LEONARD®

7777 W. BLUEMOUND RD. P.O. BOX 13819 MILWAUKEE, WI 53213

Visit Hal Leonard Online at
www.halleonard.com

Table of Contents

Using the Audio and MIDI Accompaniments

Fully orchestrated accompaniments are available for this book as MP3s and MIDI files. Throughout the book, audio tracks are indicated by this icon 🔊 1. *Practice* and *performance* tempo tracks are provided for each exercise 1–20 and for the chromatic-scale exercises at the end of the book. The audio accompaniments are available only in the book/audio package (HL00296165). Accompaniment titles, track listings and detailed instructions for using the audio accompaniments are also included with the book/audio package.

Preface

Since it first appeared in 1873, Charles-Louis Hanon's *Le Pianiste virtuose (The Virtuoso Pianist)* has become the most widely used set of etudes in the world. Hanon explained in his introduction to the book that the 60 exercises of *The Virtuoso Pianist* were designed to build "speed, precision, agility and strength of all the fingers and flexibility of the wrists." He also promised that the exercises would develop equal strength in the right and left hands. The book won the silver medal at the Exposition Universelle in 1878 and was approved for use at the Paris Conservatoire during Hanon's lifetime. The first English translation appeared in 1894. By 1900, the year of Hanon's death, the book was in use throughout Europe and the United States. The book is still in use today by piano students and professional performers in both the classical and pop worlds. The exercises are also widely used in transcriptions for guitar and accordion, and the simple pattern repetitions that characterize Hanon's exercises have been imitated in contemporary piano studies, such as *Jazz Hanon* and *Salsa Hanon*.

Charles-Louis Hanon

Charles-Louis Hanon was born on July 2, 1819 in the French town of Renescure, near Dunkerque. His father was a musician and schoolmaster. In 1846, Hanon became the organist and choir director at Eglise Saint-Joseph in Boulogne-sur-mer, a town not far from Renescure. He was dismissed from this job in 1853 but stayed in Boulonge, living with his brother and a friend named Louis Légier. Here he composed, published his own music, taught piano and voice, and rented out pianos. His publications include a collection of 12 pieces entitled *Les Délices des jeunes pianistes* (Delights of Young Pianists) and the *Six fantaisias élégantes sur les plus beaux motifs de Bellini et Rossini* (Six Elegant Fantasies on the Most Beautiful Motives of Bellini and Rossini). He also wrote hymns and popular songs in addition to other methods.

Hanon's real gift seems to have been for teaching. In addition to the 60 progressive studies of *The Virtuoso Pianist* he also published a four-volume complete method for organ in 1863-68, and a beginning harmony book in 1873. He died of pneumonia on March 19, 1900. Today, more than 100 years after his death, his name and the 60 etudes of *The Virtuoso Pianist* are known throughout the world. One of very few nineteenth-century piano methods still in use, it continues to shape and polish the playing of yet another generation of pianists.

– *Elaine Schmidt*

General Practice Tips

- In each exercise, *Parts A* and *B* are made up of one-measure patterns that are repeated on different starting notes. To become familiar with each pattern before actually playing it, tap it on the closed lid of the piano or on a flat surface away from the keyboard.

- Prepare for each new exercise by doing the activities suggested on the study page with your teacher.

- Each exercise has two sections: *Part A* and *Part B*. Begin by practicing *Part A* and *Part B* as two separate exercises, hands alone at first, then hands together. Use the optional ending in the music for *Part A*. When you can play each part confidently hands together, combine the two into one continuous exercise, omitting the optional ending for *Part A*.

- Keep a steady pulse from beginning to end, using a metronome as you practice. Begin with your metronome set at ♩ = 60. When you can play the exercise comfortably at that speed, steadily increase your practice tempo by setting your metronome at a gradually faster pace (♩ = 72, 84, etc.) with ♩ = 120 as your goal.

- Keep your fingers close to the keys as you play. Curve your fingers and support them with a relaxed but rounded hand position, and a level wrist.

- Balance the weight of your arm over each finger as you move smoothly from finger to finger.

- Play with a full, distinct sound. Let your ear act as a teacher for your fingers. Listening carefully to the sound that you make will help you create a full rich tone, one that is smooth and even throughout.

- When playing hands together, be sure that the right-hand and left-hand notes sound at exactly the same time.

- When you can play the entire exercise confidently at ♩ = 120, you are ready to apply the performance suggestions in the *Virtuoso Variations*.

- In addition to the specific *Virtuoso Variations* suggested for each exercise throughout the book, create your own original 'virtuoso variations' using combinations of rhythms, dynamics, and articulations. Have fun!

A Note to the Teacher

The practice suggestions in this edition reflect a contemporary approach to piano technique that emphasizes *interdependence* of the fingers, hand, wrist and arm. Hanon's exercises, when approached from this standpoint, aptly fulfill their author's original intention. That is, they are excellent studies for the development of agility, rhythmic precision, and an evenly balanced sound. We recommend that upon mastering this volume, students progress to the original *G. Schirmer* edition to further develop their technique and to discover these classic studies as Hanon originally conceived them.

Margaret Otwell

Theory Basics

In the *Quick Quiz* section of each worksheet, you will be asked to identify intervals, triads, and chord inversions. The reference chart below defines these important concepts.

Intervals

An **interval** is the distance from one key to another key on the keyboard, and from one note to another note on the staff.

Intervals are counted beginning with the first note indicated, and ending with the second note. For example, in the chart below, the distance from C to E is a 3rd because you have counted the notes C-D-E.

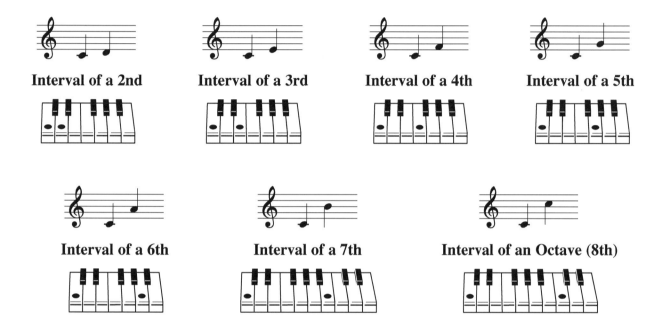

Interval of a 2nd   **Interval of a 3rd**   **Interval of a 4th**   **Interval of a 5th**

Interval of a 6th   **Interval of a 7th**   **Interval of an Octave (8th)**

Triads and Inversions

A triad can have three positions: *root position*, *first inversion*, or *second inversion*. The lowest note of the chord determines the position of the chord.

When a chord is inverted, the lowest note and the intervals that form the chord change, but the note names remain the same:

Exercise One

Mastering the ability to play the interval of a third easily, using fingers 4 and 5.

Practice Tips

- Stretching between fingers 4 and 5 in each hand is easy if you let your wrist and arm follow your fingers as you play.
- Keep the weight of your arm balanced over each finger as you play.
- Keep your wrist flexible, using it to help transfer the weight of your arm from finger to finger as you move up or down on the keyboard.
- Focus on fingers 4 and 5 by practicing the warm-ups below. Practice these and all other warm-ups throughout the book slowly, with a smooth, *legato* touch.

(Part A)

(Part B)

Quick Quiz

1. Play the first note and the last note in the excerpt below.

   Name the interval between these two notes. _____

(Part A, m. 1)

2. Play the first two notes in the same excerpt. Name the interval between these two notes. _____
3. In measure 1 of the exercise, circle the interval of a third on each staff, and the corresponding fingering in each hand.
4. In measure 8, circle the interval of a third on each staff, and the corresponding fingering in each hand.

Virtuoso Variations

- Play the entire exercise hands together, using a *staccato* touch throughout.
- Memorize the patterns in *Parts A* and *B*, then play both parts with your eyes closed. Listen carefully to the sound you create.

Part A 🔊 **1**

5

7a
Part A ending

Omit when continuing to Part B

Part B 🔊 **2**

8

12

🔊 **3** *Part A* and *Part B* combined, omitting optional *Part A* ending.

Exercise Two

Building strength and control of fingers 3 and 4.

Practice Tips

- Although this exercise begins with the same notes as Exercise One, it uses a *different* set of L.H. fingerings: 5-3, not 5-4. Practice this new finger combination in the warm-up to the right.

(Part A)

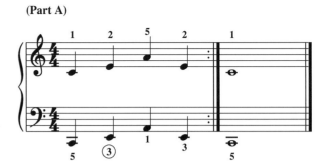

- Focus on strengthening fingers 3 and 4 in the warm-ups below. Let the full weight of your arm shift back and forth between each finger.

(Part A)

(Part B)

Quick Quiz

1. In the excerpt below, what is the interval between the first and last notes? _____
2. What is the interval between the first two notes? _____

(Part A, m. 1)

3. These notes outline a chord in first inversion. Name the root of the chord. _____
4. Play the first three R.H. notes in *each* measure of *Part A*, ending with measure 7a.
   The interval pattern will remain the same as your hand position moves up by step in each measure.

(Part A)

5. Play the first three L.H. notes in each measure of *Part A* in the same way.

Recognizing the first-inversion chords in each measure makes it easier to learn Exercise Two quickly and play it with confidence. Look for similar patterns as you progress through the book.

Virtuoso Variations

- Play *legato*, hands together, using the rhythmic variations below.

6 *Part A* and *Part B* combined, omitting optional *Part A* ending.

Exercise Three

Strengthening the inner fingers (2-3-4) of each hand.

Practice Tips

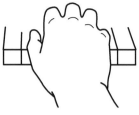

- As in Exercise Two, the patterns in Exercise Three begin with first-inversion chords and fingerings.
- Curve your fingers so that you can see only the middle joint of your fingers as you practice. If you can see your fingernails as you play, your fingers are probably not rounded enough.
- Play as smoothly and clearly as possible, letting the weight of your arm move from finger to finger as you play. Focus on this skill in the warm-ups below.

(Part A)

(Part A)

Quick Quiz

1. In the excerpt below, do the notes outline a chord in *root position* or in *first inversion*? _____

2. Name the root of the chord. _____

(Part B, m. 8)

3. Play the first three L.H. notes in *each* measure of *Part B*.

(Part B)

etc.

4. Play the first three R.H. notes in each measure of *Part B* in the same way.

5. Compare the patterns in Exercises Two and Three. How are the last four notes of each measure alike? How are they different?

Virtuoso Variations

- Play hands together, alternating *legato* and *staccato* measures throughout (for example: measure 1 *legato*; measure 2 *staccato*; measure 3 *legato;* etc.).
- Select dynamics and add them to the variation above.

9 *Part A* and *Part B* combined, omitting optional *Part A* ending.

Exercise Four

Strengthening the outer fingers (4-5) of each hand.

Practice Tips

- Keep your wrist flexible, and transfer the weight of your arm from the inner to the outer fingers of your hand as you play.

- Think of the large muscle at the outside edge of your hand as an extension of your fifth finger. Use this muscle to help fingers 4 and 5 play with strength.

- Keep a good hand position as you play fingers 4 and 5, being careful not to tip your hand over to one side. Practice this skill in the warm-ups below.

(Part A)

(Part B)

- In *Part A*, R.H. finger 2 must shift from D to E, while in *Part B*, L.H. finger 3 extends to play the interval of a fourth. These shifts help you to move your hand easily into place for the next notes in the pattern. Focus on this new skill in the warm-ups below.

(Part A)

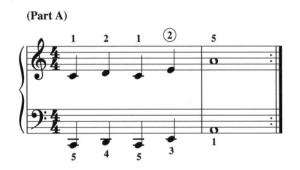

(Part B)

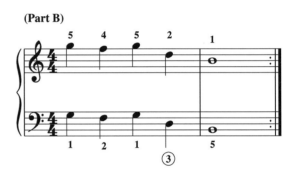

Quick Quiz

In the following excerpts, name the intervals indicated by the brackets.

(Part A, m. 1)

(Part B, m. 8)

Virtuoso Variations

- Play *legato,* hands together, using the rhythmic variations below.

1. ♪♪♪♪ ♩ ♩ ♩ ♩   2. ♩ ♩ ♩ ♩ ♪♪♪♪

- Play *Part A piano* throughout, and *Part B forte* throughout.

12 *Part A* and *Part B* combined, omitting optional *Part A* ending.

Exercise Five

Transferring the weight of the arm evenly over all the fingers of the hand.

Practice Tips

- Keep the weight of your arm balanced directly over each finger as you play.
- Be careful to keep your hand from tipping over to one side when you play finger 5.
- Play with the outside tip of your thumb. Remember this saying: *"Make a C, not a V,"* to help keep a good thumb position as you play.

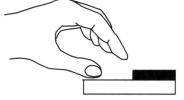

(Part A)

- In *Part A*, the notes on beats 2, 3, and 4 move down by step to beat 1 in the next measure. As you practice the warm-up to the right, feel how your fingers 'walk down' by step on each beat.

- Compare measure 1 to measure 8. Notice how the patterns in *Part A* look and feel quite different from the patterns in *Part B*. This is the first exercise in which the *Part B* pattern is not an exact mirror image, or inversion, of *Part A*.

(Part B)

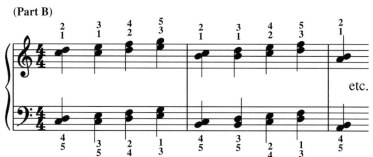

- Practice *Part B* in blocked intervals. This will help you learn the descending pattern easily.

(Part B, m. 1)

Quick Quiz

1. In the excerpt to the right, name the intervals indicated by the brackets.

2. Circle the last two notes in the excerpt. Name the interval between these two notes. _____

Virtuoso Variations

- Play hands together, first *legato*, and then *staccato*, using the rhythmic variations below.

Exercise Six

Strengthening finger 5 as it alternates with all the other fingers of the hand.

Practice Tips

- Play with a full, rich tone and listen carefully for each note to sound at exactly the same time.
- Let the weight of your arm rock slightly back and forth between the repeating finger (1 or 5) and the other fingers of your hand. As you increase the tempo, decrease the rocking motion, keeping the weight of your arm balanced evenly across your entire hand position in each measure.
- Curve your fingers and keep the bridge of your hand arched. Keeping a good arch as you play allows your fingers to move freely from the bridge of your hand.
- Practice *Part A* and *Part B* in blocked intervals in the warm-ups below. As you play, remember to keep the bridge of your hand gently firm and your fingers curved.

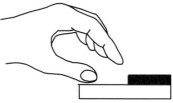

Keep a good arch.

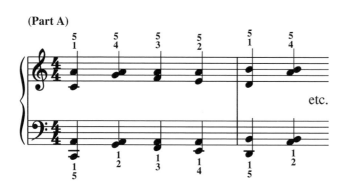

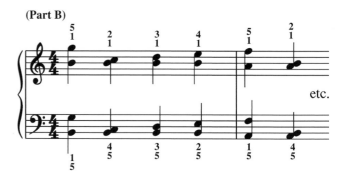

Quick Quiz

1. In the following excerpts, name the intervals indicated by the brackets.

2. How are these interval patterns different from those in Exercise Five?

Virtuoso Variations

- Play hands together, using the variations below.
  Be certain to lift off at the end of each slur in the first variation.

18 *Part A* and *Part B* combined, omitting optional *Part A* ending.

Exercise Seven

Strengthening the outer fingers (3-4-5) of the hand.
Contracting the hand by placing fingers 1 and 3 on adjacent keys.

Practice Tips

- In Exercises One through Six, your hand position expands to a sixth to play the interval patterns. Exercise Seven teaches the equally valuable skill of contracting, or "closing," your hand position while playing.

- Fingers 1 and 3 *always* play the contractions, but at *different* times in each hand. To become comfortable with this new coordination challenge, tap the contraction patterns hands together on the closed lid of the keyboard or on a tabletop away from the piano. This symbol (1 ——▸ 3) indicates the finger contractions.

Tap, hands together:

R.H.	3	5	4	3	——▸	1
L.H.	3	1 ——▸ 3	4	5		

- Practice the warm-ups below, hands alone and then together, until you are comfortable contracting fingers 1 and 3 in both hands.

(Part A)

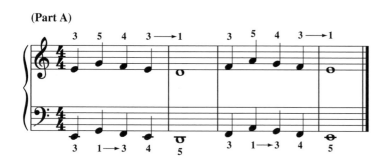

(Part B)

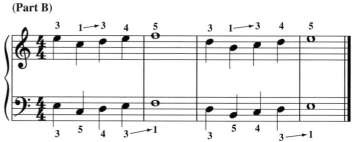

- Practice Exercise Seven in blocked intervals, ascending and descending, pairing the eighth notes in each measure.

(Part A)

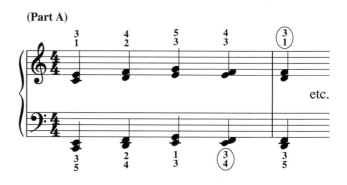

etc.

Quick Quiz

1. In the excerpt to the right, name the intervals indicated by the brackets.

(Part A, m. 8)

Virtuoso Variations

- Play hands together, using the articulation variations below.

1.

2.

21 *Part A* and *Part B* combined, omitting optional *Part A* ending.

Exercise Eight

Stretching easily between finger 2 and fingers 4-5.
Balancing the weight of the arm evenly over each finger.

Practice Tips

- Pay careful attention to the L.H. fingering 5-4 that begins each measure in *Part A*, and the R.H. fingering 5-4 that begins each measure in *Part B*.

- Stretching between finger 2 and fingers 4-5 in each hand is easy if you let your wrist and hand follow your fingers as you play. Imagine 'walking' comfortably on curved fingers from note to note, centering your arm weight over each finger that plays. As you increase the tempo, think of 'running' on your fingers across the keys.

- Keep your wrist flexible. Locking your wrist will prevent you from transferring the weight of your arm to each finger as you play. Practice each warm-up below hands together.

(Part A)

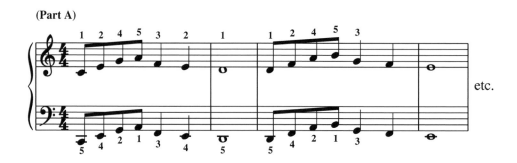

etc.

(Part B)

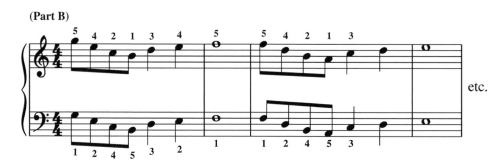

etc.

Quick Quiz

Play the first three R.H. notes in *Part A*, measure 1.

1. What major triad is outlined by these three notes? _____
2. How many major triads can you find in *Part A*? _____ In *Part B*? _____

Using the triads in each measure, create your own warm-ups for Exercise Eight.

Virtuoso Variations

- Play hands together, using the articulation variations below.

1. 　　　　　2.

24 *Part A* and *Part B* combined, omitting optional *Part A* ending.

Exercise Nine

Balancing the weight of the arm over each finger of the hand.

Practice Tips

- When stretching between fingers 4 and 5 in Exercise Nine, let your wrist and hand follow your fingers as you play.
- In *Part A*, the notes on beats 2, 3, and 4 move up by step as you gradually shift the weight of your arm from the thumb to finger 5. In *Part B*, the notes on these same beats move down by step. Practice the warm-ups below, focusing on 'walking up' by step in *Part A*, and 'walking down' by step in *Part B*. Play *legato* and listen for a smooth, even sound.

(Part A)

etc.

(Part B)

etc.

Quick Quiz

1. In the following excerpts, name the intervals indicated by the brackets.

(Part A, m. 1)

(Part B, m. 8)

2. What is the interval between the lowest and the highest notes in each excerpt? _____

Virtuoso Variations

- Practice hands together, *forte*, using this articulation variation below.

- Practice hands together, *piano*, letting your wrist rebound lightly on each note as you play.

27 *Part A* and *Part B* combined, omitting optional *Part A* ending.

Exercise Ten

Strengthening the finger pairs 2-3 and especially, 3-4. Trill preparation.

Practice Tips

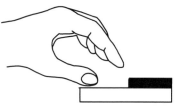

Keep a good arch.

- Keep your wrist flexible, using it to help transfer the weight of your arm from finger to finger as you play.
- Curve your fingers and keep the bridge of your hand arched and gently firm.
- For a good thumb position remember this saying: *"Make a C, not a V."*
- Focus on these skills in the following warm-ups.

(Part A)

(Part B)

- Practice Exercise Ten in blocked intervals, hands together, *Parts A and B.*

Quick Quiz

1. In the excerpt below, circle the three notes that outline the A minor chord.

(Part A, m. 1)

2. Play the A minor chord in blocked form, using the R.H. fingering indicated.

3. Is this a *root-position*, or *first-inversion* chord? _____

Virtuoso Variations

- Play hands together, using the rhythmic variations below.

1. [rhythmic notation]   2. [rhythmic notation]

- Play hands together, in even eighth notes, R.H. *legato* and L.H. *staccato*. Then reverse.

Exercise Eleven

Strengthening the finger pair 4-5. Trill preparation.

Practice Tips

- Keep your fingers curved and firm, but not rigid, as you play.
- Play each note with a full, evenly matched sound.
- Avoid any blurring of sound, especially between fingers 3, 4, and 5.
- Keep your wrist flexible and level, being careful not to tip it over to one side as you play fingers 4 and 5. Focus on these skills in the warm-ups below.

(Part A)

(Part B)

Quick Quiz

1. In the following excerpts, name the root of each outlined chord.

(Part A, m. 1)

_____

(Part B, m. 8)

_____

2. Do the notes in both excerpts outline a *first-* or *second-inversion* chord? _____

Virtuoso Variations

- Play hands together, using the articulation variations below. Be sure to lift off at the end of each slur.

- Select dynamics and add them to the variations above.

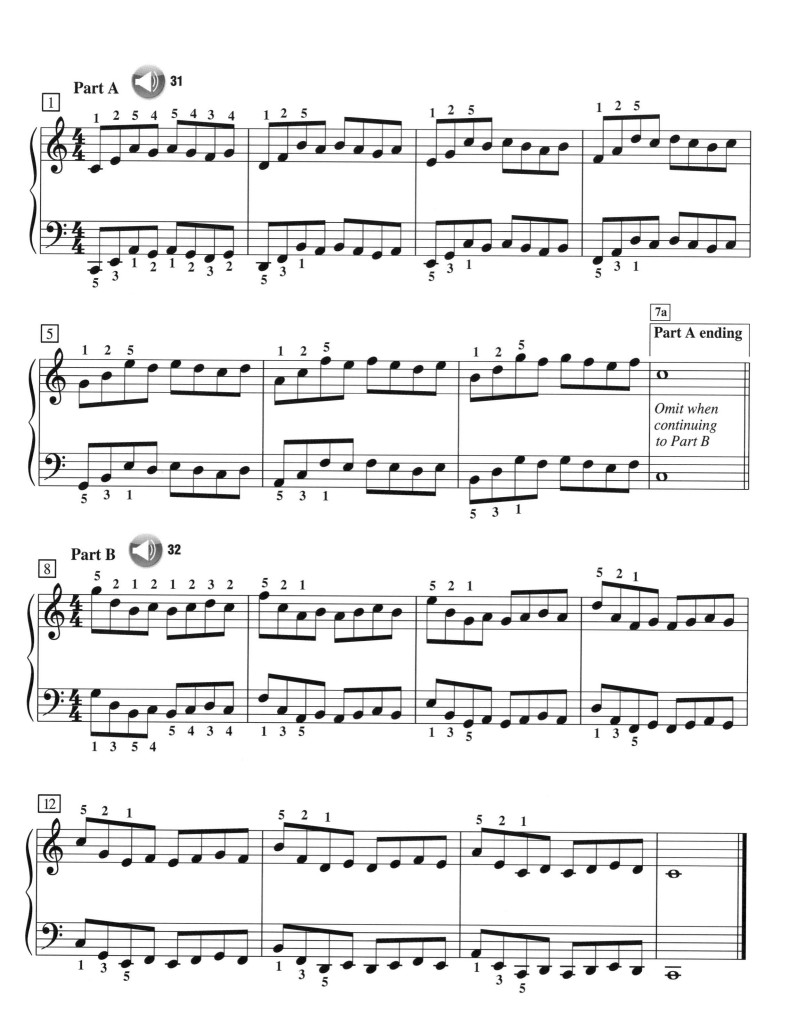

33 *Part A* and *Part B* combined, omitting optional *Part A ending.*

Exercise Twelve

Extending fingers 1 and 5. Strengthening fingers 3, 4, and 5.

Practice Tips

- Exercise Twelve introduces the interval of the seventh for the first time in this book.
- Listen carefully to avoid any blurring or overlapping of sound, especially between fingers 3, 4, and 5.
- Play each note with a full, evenly-matched sound. Be careful not to accent the thumb notes.
- Practice the warm-ups below, feeling the distance of the seventh in your fingers.
  Then, repeat each warm-up with your eyes closed.

Quick Quiz

1. The first three notes of each measure in *Part A* outline a chord in first inversion. Play each L.H. chord in blocked form.
2. How many major chords did you hear? _____ How many minor chords? _____
3. Is the R.H. fingering in *Part A* the usual fingering for first-inversion chords? _____

Virtuoso Variations

- Pause on each *fermata*, balancing the weight of your hand on that note. Play the notes between each *fermata* in one quick motion, as clearly as possible.

- Shift the *fermata* to the 5th-finger notes, playing the remaining notes in each measure in one quick motion. Pause only when you reach the *fermata* on the next downbeat.

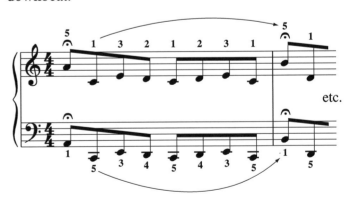

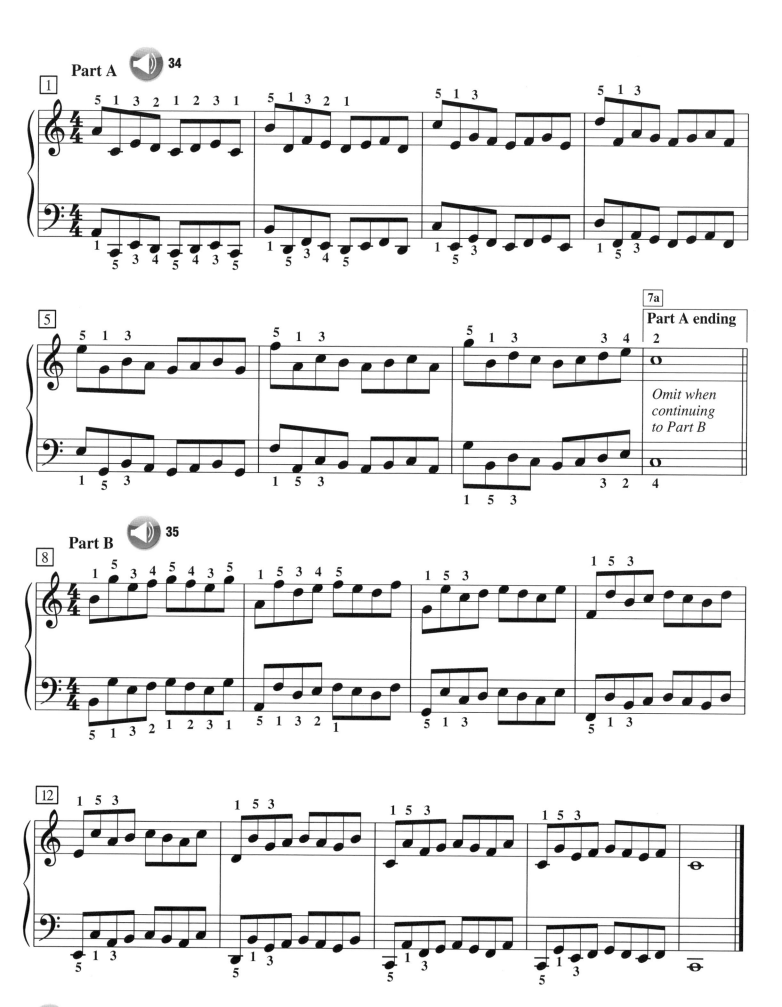

36 *Part A* and *Part B* combined, omitting optional *Part A* ending.

Exercise Thirteen

Strengthening the outer fingers (3-4-5) of the hand.
Contracting the hand by placing fingers 1 and 3, or 3 and 5, on adjacent keys.

Practice Tips

- Each measure in Exercise Thirteen remains in a five-finger pattern and requires no hand extension. However, to get from one measure to the next, your hand must contract and skip a finger (R.H. 5-3 and L.H. 1-3), so the five-finger pattern can move up or down a step to begin the new measure.

- This contraction is easy to play hands together because the third fingers in both hands always land on the same note at the same time. Focus on this skill by practicing the warm-ups below. Each time you play finger 3, say "three" aloud.

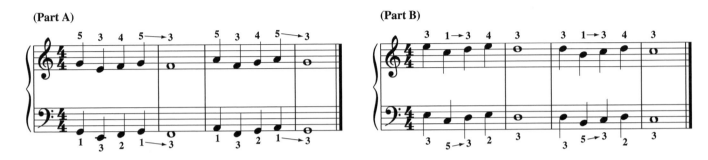

Quick Quiz

1. In the following excerpt, name the intervals indicated by the brackets.

(Part A, m. 1)

Virtuoso Variations

- Play hands together, using the variations below in each measure.

- Create your own variation of this exercise using blocked intervals.

39 *Part A* and *Part B* combined, omitting optional *Part A* ending.

Exercise Fourteen

Strengthening the finger pairs 3-4. Trill preparation.
Contracting the hand by placing fingers 1 and 3, or 1 and 4, on adjacent keys.

Practice Tips

- As in Exercise Thirteen, each measure in Exercise Fourteen remains in a five-finger position. However, the hand contractions do *not* occur at the same time in the measure.
- In *Part A*, the R.H. contraction occurs *over* the barline (4-1) and the L.H. contraction occurs just *before* the barline (1-3). Focus on this coordination challenge in the *Part A* warm-up below. Practice hands alone, then hands together.
- In *Part B*, the R.H. contraction occurs just *before* the barline (1-3) and the L.H. contraction occurs *over* the barline (4-1). Practice these contractions in the *Part B* warm-up below. Practice hands alone, then hands together.

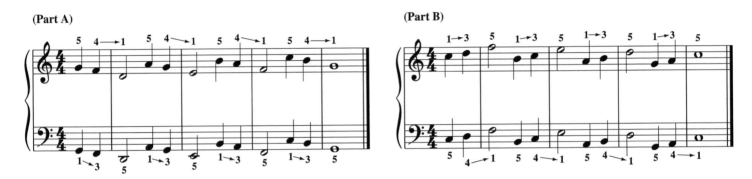

- After you have learned Exercise Fourteen with the fingering indicated, experiment with this alternate fingering: Use fingers 1-2 in the L.H. *Part A* and R.H. *Part B* on the last beat of each measure (instead of 1-3). This fingering choice poses less of a coordination challenge between the hands because the contractions now occur at the *same* time in each measure.

Quick Quiz

1. In the following excerpt, identify the seconds in brackets as half steps (H) or whole steps (W).

(Part A, m. 1-2)

2. Is the pattern of whole steps and half steps the same in both measures? _____

Virtuoso Variations

- Play hands together, using the variations below in each measure.

42 *Part A* and *Part B* combined, omitting optional *Part A* ending.

Exercise Fifteen

Strengthening fingers 1-2-3-4-5.

Practice Tips

- Exercise Fifteen is the first exercise in which you must shift your thumb to a new key *within* the pattern. This shift enables your hand to move into position for the next measure.

- Follow the fingering exactly, resisting the temptation to play thirds with 1-3 where 1-2 is indicated. Focus on this new skill by practicing the warm-ups below.

(Part A)

1.

(Part B)

2.

(Part A)

3.

(Part B)

4.

Quick Quiz

1. The two measures in Exercise Fifteen that end with the interval of a second are: m. _____ and m. _____.

2. In the excerpt below, name the interval between the first and last notes in the first measure. _____

(Part B, m. 8-9)

3. Name the interval between the last two notes in this excerpt. _____

Virtuoso Variations

- Play the R.H. as written while the L.H. plays in blocked thirds.

- Then, reverse and play the R.H. in blocked thirds while the L.H. plays as written.

- For a challenging "double twist," play these same variations with R.H. *legato* and L.H. *staccato*. Then, reverse the articulations in each hand.

45 *Part A* and *Part B* combined, omitting optional *Part A* ending.

Exercise Sixteen

Stretching between R.H. 3 and 5. Strengthening fingers 3-4-5.

Practice Tips

- Throughout the exercise, be sure to keep your arm weight evenly balanced over each finger.

- In *Part A*, keep your R.H. wrist flexible and level, being careful not to tip it over to one side when stretching from finger 3 to finger 5. Focus on this skill in the warm-up to the right.

- Avoid any overlapping or blurring of sound, especially between fingers 3-4-5. Listen carefully as you practice the following warm-ups.

(Part A)

(Part B)

Quick Quiz

1. In the following excerpts, name the intervals indicated by the brackets.

(Part A, m. 1)

(Part B, m. 8)

Virtuoso Variations

- Play hands together, using the rhythmic variation below.

- In this variation, release each slur with a slight upward motion of your wrist, relaxing your hands on each rest.

- Create your own original virtuoso variations using combinations of rhythms, dynamics, and articulations.

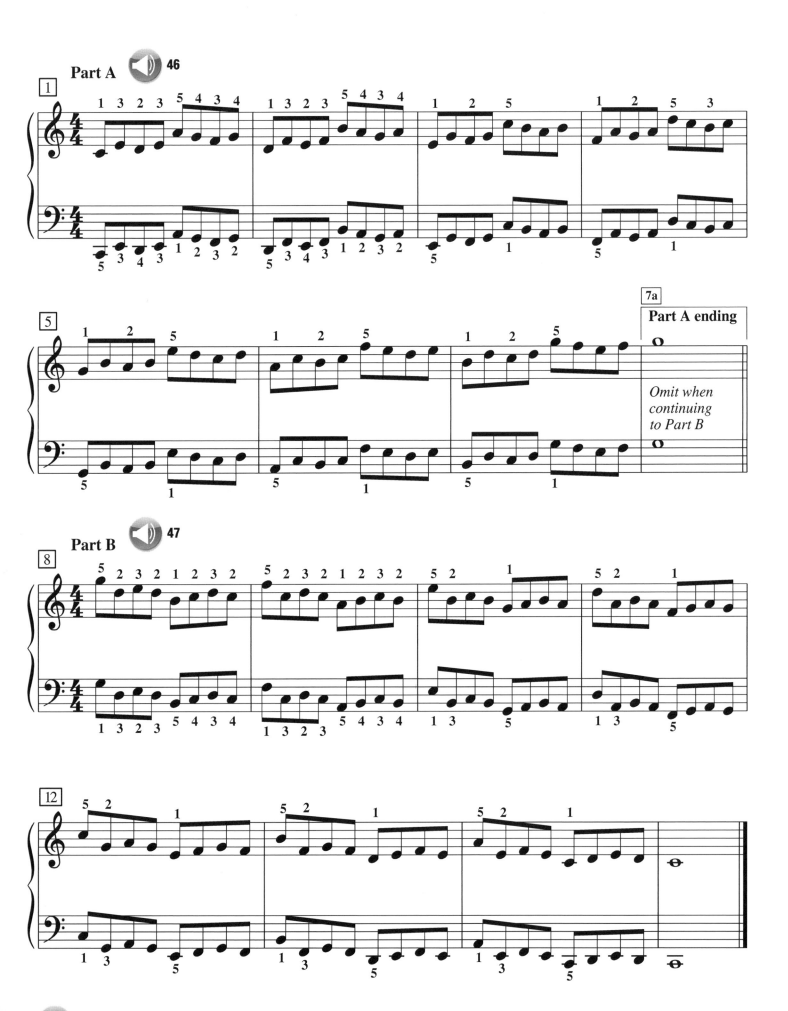

48 *Part A* and *Part B* combined, omitting optional *Part A* ending.

Exercise Seventeen

Extending the hand position by stretching between several fingers.

Practice Tips

- Keep your wrists flexible and your arms and shoulders relaxed, balancing the weight of your arm over each finger.
- Play with curved fingers, using the large muscle on the outside of your hand to support fingers 4 and 5.
- As you move toward finger 5, roll forward slightly on the pads of your fingers, shifting your arm weight smoothly to finger 5. Let your thumb follow your hand. Once you have played finger 5, shift your weight back and continue on. Practice these important skills in the following warm-ups.

(Part A)

(Part B)

- As you play Exercise Seventeen, be sure to move smoothly and without hesitation through the bar lines.

Quick Quiz

1. Name the root of each first-inversion chord in the following excerpts: _____ and _____

(Part A, m. 1)

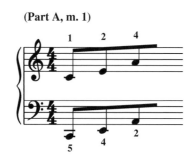

(Part B, m. 8)

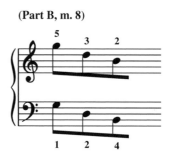

2. How is the fingering in these excerpts different from the usual L.H. and R.H. fingering for first-inversion chords?

3. Play the last four notes in measure 1 (*Part A*), and in measure 8 (*Part B*). Are the intervals the same? _____

Virtuoso Variations

- Play hands together, using the variations below.

51 *Part A* and *Part B* combined, omitting optional *Part A* ending.

Exercise Eighteen

Contraction of the hand by placing 1 and 3, or 3 and 5, on adjacent keys.
Strengthening all the fingers of the hand.

Practice Tips

- To move from one measure to the next, you must contract your hand at the end of each measure so that finger 5 or finger 1 is in place to begin the pattern again. Before playing the exercise, practice the contraction in the following warm-ups hands alone, then together.

(Part A)

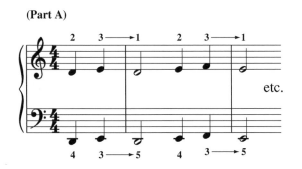

etc.

(Part B)

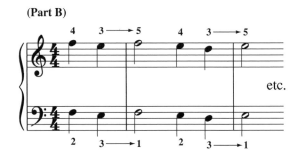

etc.

Quick Quiz

1. Circle all the seconds in each excerpt below.
2. Name the interval that separates each second. _____

(Part A, m. 1)

(Part B, m. 8)

3. Are the seconds in *Part B* a mirror image of *Part A*? _____
4. What major root-position triad lies within each excerpt above? _____
5. Find and play the root-position triads in measures 1-7 and 8-13 in Exercise Eighteen.

Virtuoso Variations

- Play *Part A* in contrary motion. Begin with both thumbs on Middle C, and use the R.H. fingering for both hands.
- In this variation, pause on each *fermata*, balancing the weight of your hand on that note. Play the notes between each *fermata* in one quick motion, as clearly as possible.

- Create your own variation using blocked intervals.

54 *Part A* and *Part B* combined, omitting optional *Part A* ending.

Exercise Nineteen

Strengthening all the fingers of the hand.

Practice Tips

- The note pattern in Exercise Nineteen changes direction several times within the measure, producing a swirling 'windmill' effect when played at a fast tempo. Aim for beats 1 and 3, and feel the weight of your arm shift between your thumb and the outer part of your hand as you play.

- Practice the R.H. warm-ups below. Pause on each *fermata*, and play the notes between the *fermatas* in one smooth motion.

- Practice slowly at first, with a full tone and *legato* touch. Then, increase your speed, using one quick motion to play each group of four eighth notes. Listen for an even, flowing sound.

- Using these warm-ups as a model, practice the L.H. in *Parts A* and *B* the same way.

Quick Quiz

1. In the excerpt from *Part A* below, do the notes outline a *first-* or *second-inversion* chord? _____

2. Name the root of this chord. _____

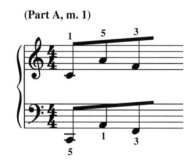

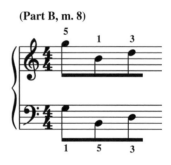

3. In the excerpt from *Part B* above, do the notes outline a *first-* or *second-inversion* chord? _____

4. Which hand uses the usual fingering for the chord inversion in *Part A*? _____ In *Part B*? _____

Virtuoso Variations

- Play hands together, using the variations below in each measure.

57 *Part A* and *Part B* combined, omitting optional *Part A* ending.

Exercise Twenty

Extending to an octave. Strengthening fingers 2, 3, and 4.

Practice Tips

- In this exercise, extending your hand position to reach an octave is made easier because fingers 2 and 4 play the two chord tones in between the octave notes.

- Keep your wrists flexible and your arms and shoulders relaxed. Imagine 'walking' comfortably on curved fingers from note to note, centering your arm weight over each finger that plays. As you increase the tempo, move quickly from note to note, as if your fingers were 'running' across the keys.

- To feel the intervals played by fingers 1-2-4-5 and 5-4-2-1 in *Part A*, slowly practice the warm-up to the right, hands alone, then hands together.

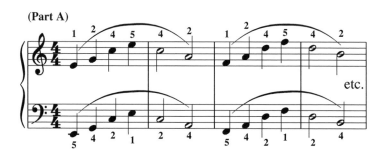

(Part A)

- In *Part B*, although the third and fifth notes in each measure are the same, they are played with different fingers because your hand must contract to continue. Focus on this contraction in the warm-up to the right.

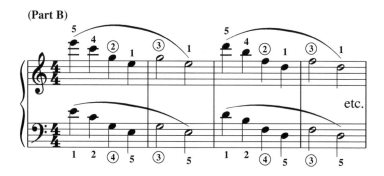

(Part B)

- When moving from measure 8 to measure 9, you must transfer the weight of your arm from R.H. finger 2 to finger 5. Play with a flexible wrist, and roll slightly forward on the tip of finger 2 to play finger 5 with ease.

Quick Quiz

1. What is the interval between the first and fourth notes in each excerpt below? _____

2. Circle the first three notes in the excerpt from *Part A*. Name this first-inversion chord. _____

(Part A, m. 1)   (Part B, m. 9)

3. Compare the last four notes in each excerpt.
   Are the intervals in these patterns the same? _____ Are the interval directions the same? _____

Virtuoso Variations

- Play hands together, using the variations below.

58

Part A

8a
Part A ending

Omit when continuing to Part B

59

Part B

60 *Part A* and *Part B* combined, omitting optional *Part A* ending.

Chromatic Scales

Hands separate

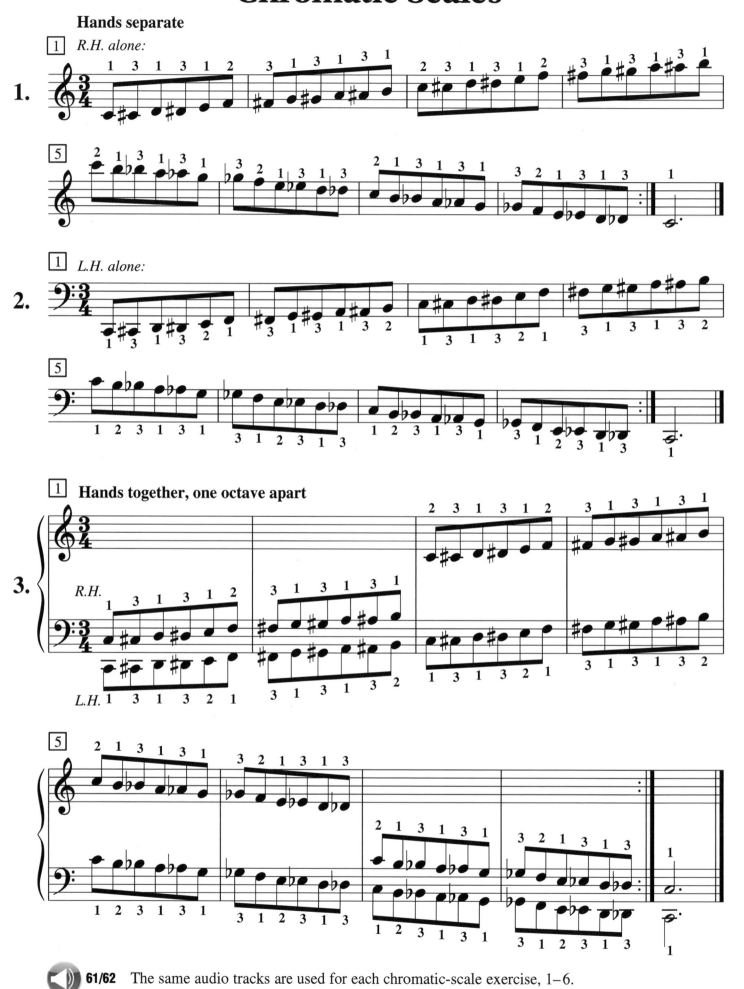

61/62 The same audio tracks are used for each chromatic-scale exercise, 1–6.

61/62 The same audio tracks are used for each chromatic-scale exercise, 1–6.

47

Hands together in contrary motion, beginning on the major 3rd 61/62

(The same fingers in each hand play at the same time.)

Alternate fingering, often used for *legato* passages 63/64